The World From X to Z

Celeste Roselli

BookLeaf Publishing
India | USA | UK

Presentation by *BookLeaf Publishing*

Web: www.bookleafpub.com

E-mail: info@bookleafpub.com

ISBN: 9789363301368

First edition 2024

To my amazingly large and perfect family, for encouraging the ramblings of a really talkative kid.

To my Nana, for everything; most of all, for defining strength.

To Henry, for never failing to make me start laughing during a late-night existential crisis.

PREFACE

I completed this book as a part of a writing challenge where I was tasked to write poetry every single day for 21 days, around one entry per day. After the 21 days ended, my editing privileges would as well. As a complete perfectionist, this scared the crap out of me, and I think having the crap scared out of you is the perfect way to start writing. Why do you think this book is full of so many existential crises, huh?

So, as I anxiously hit submit on this book on my 21st day, I'm reminded of Billy Joel's famous lyric from Vienna: "but don't you know that only fools are satisfied?" It seems counter-intuitive that writing a poetry collection about searching for the meaning of life would teach me to simply relax and hit submit, but life is full of weird phenomena, so I'm not that surprised. (Don't worry, I still did a final grammar check.) Finally, I hope you enjoy reading this crazy, impulsive experiment as much I as enjoyed writing it.

Physics Textbook

There is a wonder as I sit in physics,
a heartfelt longing when I see the stars;
there is the endless question of our universe,
and there's a pain in knowing you're too small.

There is a sadness in unanswered queries,
in lifetimes cut too short to see the ligh-

-and there's a joy attempting understanding,
in inching ever closer to a why;
this is the fuel that keeps me burning questions:
if I won't ever know, at least I'll try.

Spiraled Scripture

Class in session, schedule sticks
Clock moves standardly in ticks
one two three five eight thirteen
(Can someone tell me what this means?)

Sequence spirals from the ink
Math on paper makes me think
Is there a greater force that leads
My pen to chart the frame of leaves

And not just leaves, my face proportioned!
Faith is fickle, math is certain
Trace the curves of shells on beaches
Pastors talk, but cell shape preaches

Patterns build, my thoughts are scattered
"Meaningless" perceptions shattered
These ratios multiply like rabbits:
It's in the grass that they inhabit

You can preach that there's no god
Or that there's only one to see
But my conviction stands with this:
The scripture written in the trees

Magnetic

Pinning to the fridge
Tying rocks to tides
Balancing the bridge
Life's invisible guide

Stabilize the planets
Hold a force between
Past and present, big bang's indent
Marked through history

Fold the poles like lace
Press the force of fields
Tied to time and space:

I have galaxies as shields

Space Camp - A Narrative

I'm sitting underneath a rocket that is over 5,000,000 times my weight, 796 times my height. And it has traveled more miles in 48 hours than I will in a year. And I am terrified. I am terrified of something so big, something so non-understandable, something so mysterious and complicated and scientific. At only 10 years old, I don't feel like I'll ever understand the deepest parts of our world. But I guess that's what Space Camp is for: to quell the existential dread with space trivia.

"What's interesting," David, my cabin leader, says, "is that matter is one of the rarest things in our universe. At the big bang, most positrons and electrons destroyed each other. The ones that didn't became everything else. In that big bang, every single thing inside this museum, every single thing in the universe, was created from the same starting materials - including you."

He looks at us like how I assume I look at the stars: excitedly, fascinated by knowledge. "Without that little bit of luck, those few ions that didn't destroy each other, there would be no you, no rockets, no matter of any kind…" I zone out after he says that, probably talking about space history of some sort. Looking up at the ginormous rocket above me (and the ginormous rockets all around me, considering this is the Space and Rocketry Museum in Huntsville, Alabama), I'm amazed, but not amazed like seeing magic tricks. I feel understood; maybe I'm the one truly understanding for the first time.

As I stroll around the museum that day, I notice pieces of moon rock and space suits and metal from the space station - all items that have experienced the vacuum of space, which I have not. They all feel like family heirlooms.

I'm made from that rocket that is over 5,000,000 times my weight, 796 times my height. I am made from the stars it looked at as it traveled to the moon. And I realize: knowing you are the space you see makes it feel a little less scary.

Disney World

Today was the day
I discovered music, harmony, melody, can all be
explained:
It is physics, biology, and math.
As much as it seems to be so, it's not magic;
It is signals in our ears and evolutionary
preference towards consonance over dissonance
-because surprisingly, humans were safer than a
pile of falling rocks

And it reminds me of the day
I discovered that computers could all be
explained:
It is binary, light, electricity.
As much as it seems to be so, it's still not magic;
It is tiny transistors of rare metals that we create
to corral electric current from one place to
another, which in turn lights up our screens and
lit up my eyes

And I still love Disney World, but I remember
the day I learned that the characters were actors
That little bit of magic in my mind dying,
turning from belief to memory

And I guess every day at school is full of little
deaths of what we thought we knew
The world as we explained it in our minds
versus the way it explains itself
And I've always loved that, I have, I have, that
discovery, that unlocking of a secret kept from
me

So damn it, why can't I explain it this time?
And why don't I want to?
Why do I want to live in this magic and not
break it -
- take this gift from God without unwrapping it
And say I love you
No explanation needed.
I think I'll keep the magic this time

Music on the Walls - A Narrative

At 1am, one is not usually awake, creating a collage, or reading through sheet music. I, however, was doing all three. Dozens of papers strewn across the floor, I sat near a window seat and cut through Handel's Messiah (only cutting the sheet from the book, though, so the actual music stayed intact). I thought that inspiration "striking" you was a metaphor, but though I've never had the experience of being struck by lightning, this was the closest I had been to it. Ordinary paper, ordinary ink; but this could create something extraordinary.

From an otherwise organized shelf, a disorderly stack of paper called to me. I have the habit of saving dull and useless files, but I had saved these for a different reason; they were memories. Each time I picked up a piece of sheet music, I could hear the music playing inside my mind. I was back on stage; my heart was in my throat and in front of me was not a room strewn with paper but instead a concert hall, or an empty theater, or my voice teacher's studio. A stack did

not suffice to hold a collection of memories. So I
took to the scissors.

Symphony after symphony audiated in my brain
as memories flooded from each note. One sheet
was my first musical. Another stanza was the
first song I sang in a chorus of more than 250
people. I had decrypted the thick stack of
Beethoven that February, at my first national
choir conference. The snips and sticks of the
paper to my wall created the beat in which these
memories played: Cut, fold, tape. Cut, fold, tape.
No thoughts, just flowing music. Each memory,
each piece of music that only I can hear, healed
me a little bit. The papers collected on the walls
surrounding my window, stretching taller and
taller, until they covered every inch of paint
from floor to ceiling. Unique memories and
moments plastered over the pink wall that has
been there since I was six. Ordinary paper,
ordinary ink, expressed more than words can.
And I was no longer scared of forgetting.

I woke up with a melody

I woke up from a dream with a melody in my
mind
And as one who doesn't hear back from
inspiration often is wont to do, I ran to grab a
pen.
I can hear it running through my veins
But as I step to my desk, it leaps out my window
My half-awake state grasps at the glass only to
find it closed?
Can't really hear it anymore - I can only feel it
laughing behind me
Like that long-lost conversation between
someone I don't see anymore
With edges that a water-damaged brain has
caused to crinkle and fade.
Soon there is no beat in my ear except for the
cicadas outside my window.
I hope she calls me back

Ice Cream Truck

Nostalgia floats through the windows
Only cut through by my mom's yell of
"Oh look, an ice cream truck!"

I stand by the closed door
And resist the urge to fling it open

I swear the driver smiles at me
So I wish I was small -
too short to be seen through the door's window
Wish my headphones were plugged in -
so I wouldn't have heard the song
Wish I was running home with a blue-stained
tongue

Coffee Shop

Sound infiltrates a (previously) focused psyche
Which was (previously) locked into a computer screen
Crossing items off an (online) todo list
Guarded from the world with noise-canceling (and pretty-isolating) headphones

There's a family with three kids (on the level below me)
Each young enough to not be finding solace in a tablet (although I feel like that age keeps getting younger)
Instead, they talk (yell, loudly) across the table
Goofing (living) with their siblings

And I realize that I am at the age that I yearned to be (when I was theirs)
So it's weird that I'm envious (right?)
Of the kids seated below me, drinking (and spilling) their chocolate milk
Because I know have the ability to travel to a city coffee shop (on a nice summer day)
And this (freedom) is what I wanted (previously) to grow up for

And yet I don't seem to have enough of it
(freedom) to keep my mind away from my
(online) todo list

So I don't know why I (what caused me to) take
my headphones out
But I know that my todo list won't ever end
And this moment will

Parallel Universes

Cursed to live in parallel universes
Where every action causes infinite mistakes to
occur
Simultaneously
Each thought and worry and option running the
marathon of her mind
Never hitting the finish line but running,
running, running
Until they run off the side of a cliff
Belly-flopping into an ocean   stop
crying   of tears

Cursed to wonder
If every second she takes to   just
breathe   is being wasted
Knowing life is fragile, envisioning every
opportunity of it being taken away
How can she not achieve it all
In anticipation of it being over and not having
done enough

Cursed to perfection
Not by her parents or friends or family or
teacher
Not by anyone

But by herself
By her   snap out of it   mind
When you can consider every option, it is
impossible to live with a mistake
For how could you have been a bystander to
your own failure?

But living in parallel universes
also allows her to notice
the intricacies of her thoughts, her senses,
herself.
Hearing all the noise
helps her value   silence.
Constantly thinking
means she has never stopped living,
never stopped questioning,
never stopped trying.

Being aware is a curse of being alive, because
the opposite is no way to live.

Computer / Brain

This computer's like your brain, they said:
Electric signals traverse its edges, just like
yours;
Your code / dna
Tells transistors / synapses to fire
Producing output / thoughts

Brilliant -
Because now I've stolen the keyboard from God
And can write code / dna into existence.
Like Frankenstein, although now I won't cry
"It's alive"
I will cry
"It works"
Is that better?

So I keep writing code / dna
If there's a bug, it tells me once, I find the line,
(I stare at google), I correct it
The error / worry does not sound its alarm unless
there really is a mistake
And there are no false alarms;
There are always solutions

Output / thoughts do not occur without my
control
I do not let them.
I have the power to write them into existence
and can finally, finally write them out.
I'm drunk on power / relief
Because when I switch off my computer / brain
it turns off -
That's never happened before

"It works" I cry
The fully-organized, never-breaking, controlled
monster of my own creation
This computer belongs more to me than my
brain ever did
It is not alive, but it works
Is that better?

Here and There

"What's your stance on the afterlife since It
happened?"

Rubbing fingers against the couch
It's real
Senses prove there is a place beyond my head
I see myself sitting on the couch
And answer her without thinking
Either the most honest thing I will ever grasp
Or the biggest lie I will ever tell myself.

"Either way, I believe in it:
the fact she's gone
makes me more certain
like being taught in class
energy is transformed, not destroyed
it hurts she's not here
but I know she is there"

Dear God, tell me the laws of this universe carry
into the next one

Update from a cup of coffee

I spend a lot of time searching for meaning.

I think I found a little bit of it curled up with a
book,
cup of coffee perched on my windowsill,
breeze turning the pages against my will.

I'm not sure what this means. I'll think about it
later.

Playing Piano

I'm not that good at piano
My finger are like my thoughts
(They don't usually move where I plan them to)

I'm not that good at piano
And why should I be good at piano?
Life's not as simple as white and black keys
And in the face of a screwed up world
What does a simple pastime suggest?

I'm not that good at piano
Which I guess makes it easy to spend a few
hours learning a good Billy Joel song
Sight reading to muscle memory, skipping the
chasm between thought and action

I'm not that good at piano
And I like that very much

Lighthouse

No matter how much one can predict the tides,
I feared the future's arrival, its uncertain waves
That is, until I met you

When what-ifs turned to what-will-be's,
"I can't look"s turned to "hold my hand"s
I had a constant;

There was a pattern to the wind blowing me
forward,
A periodicity in the dark clouds' flashes of hope,
A rhythm in the rocking of the sea
And a beam of hope through the fog,
Even faintly, trapped in a roaring ocean:
A ray, a way out

More than two ships passing in the night;
You were my lighthouse

Backstage - A Narrative

Backstage, I am a ghost. I sit silently, observed by none, aware of every noise and step and breath. I see the people around me move silently, rushing from spot to spot. No one makes a single sound, but the hum of excitement seems to drown out any internal monologue. Energy courses through my veins, making me alert. Running through checklists in my head, I don't have time to think anyway. It's a strange feeling knowing the people around you are thinking the same things as you are, without having to say anything. Classmates, masked in black, run past me, whispering. I can't understand what they're saying; casters rolling is the only noise I make out, but I know our heartbeats have synced. My eyes drift from them to the hundreds, maybe thousands of set pieces around me. Any surface area not covered by paint cans or tape is practically nonexistent. Shoes walk slowly through the catwalks above me, desperate to blend in; even in this solemn corner, I'm not alone. The smell of tape (there is a lot of tape) and paint and empty spaces and sweat and past laughter suffocates me as I breathe it in, one last time. I would process the memories I have back here, maybe even notice the sadness I feel on my last time backstage, but I don't have time to. I'm nostalgic for a show that hasn't ended yet.

Suddenly, I'm drawn back. I tune into the faint sound of speaking onstage. Three more lines, I think. Two now. Get ready. Don't faint. What if you faint? You don't have your lines memorized. You're gonna forget them and screw it up or leave off the wrong entrance or mess with a set piece or steal another actor's line and everyone will realize you weren't cut out for this in the first place. One more line. You're fine. You know this. I force myself to step even though I can't seem to move my legs.

Light, that's the first thing I notice. The blinding spotlights would make anyone cringe, but especially in stark contrast to the darkness I just left. As my eyes start to adjust, I see the audience. Instead of faces I could identify one by one before, I see a dark blur of shuffling silhouettes. The concept of sound seems to be slightly off-kilter. Bullets fire, each step ricocheting off the dark black, tape-strewn floor (I'm telling you, there is a lot of tape). Surely everyone in the audience can notice my heart racing with my thoughts. I'm gonna forget. I'm

gonna forget. This is it. But I don't. I breathe in
deeply.

This is it. Let's go.

Skylines

Urban fireflies dance;
I feel so much older now
And home never sleeps

We are the unexplainable things

"We are a limited amount of time" - Oliver
Burkman

To be - an infinitive suggesting an infinity
Of breaths and glances and falling asleep and
waking up in the morning
In stubbing our toes on the pain of questioning it
all
Then numbing it with Netflix

Time - a noun tearing down that infinity
Record it, hoard it, file it away to be used at a
later date
Even though later - an adverb - is as
"guaranteed" as time itself;
Grasping at sand on the beach while it falls
through our fingers

Limited - an adjective, magically conveying
humanity in just one word
But who knew exile from Eden was a gift not a
curse
Unlike us, even unaware of an end, she chose
the apple

Because some pain is worth knowing
And life is worth living
And time is worth wasting